TRIAL JURIES
AND GRAND JURIES

JEREMY P. MORLOCK

PowerKiDS
press.

NEW YORK

Published in 2020 by The Rosen Publishing Group, Inc.
29 East 21st Street, New York, NY 10010

Editor: Jane Katirgis
Book Design: Rachel Rising

Photo Credits: Cover Image Source/Photodisc/Getty Images; Cover, pp. 1, 3, 4, 5, 6, 7, 8, 9, 10, 11, 12, 13, 14, 15, 16, 17, 18, 19, 20, 21, 22, 23, 24, 25, 26, 27, 28, 29, 30, 31, 32 (background) Allgusak/Shutterstock.com; p. 5 Jim Arbogast/Photodisc/Getty Images; p. 7 Paul Morigi/Getty Images Entertainment/Getty Images; pp. 8, 15 sirtravelalot/Shutterstock.com; pp. 9, 25 Courtesy of the Library of Congress; p. 11 Popperfoto/Getty Images; pp. 11, 14, 18, 20, 24 (gavel) AVA Bitter/Shutterstock.com; p. 13 Bettman/Getty Images; p. 17 New York Daily News Archive/Contributor/Getty Images; p. 19 a katz/Shutterstock.com; p. 21 Bettmann/Contributor/Getty Images; p. 22 moodboard/Brand X Pictures/Getty Images; p. 23 POOL/AFP/Getty Images; p. 24 iQoncept/Shutterstock.com; p. 27 Boston Globe/Contributor/Getty Images; p. 29 DAVID J. PHILLIP/Staff/Getty Images; p. 30 Evgenyi/Shutterstock.com.

Library of Congress Cataloging-in-Publication Data

Names: Morlock, Jeremy, author.
Title: Trial juries and grand juries / Jeremy P. Morlock.
Description: New York : PowerKids Press, 2020. | Series: Court is in session
   | Includes index.
Identifiers: LCCN 2018027782| ISBN 9781538343340 (library bound) | ISBN
   9781538343326 (pbk.) | ISBN 9781538343333 (6 pack)
Subjects: LCSH: Jury—United States—Juvenile literature. | Trial
   practice--United States--Juvenile literature. | Grand jury—United
   States—Juvenile literature.
Classification: LCC KF9680 .M67 2019 | DDC 347.73/752—dc23
LC record available at https://lccn.loc.gov/2018027782

Manufactured in the United States of America

CPSIA Compliance Information: Batch #CSPK19. For further information contact Rosen Publishing, New York, New York at 1-800-237-9932.

Contents

THE JURY SYSTEM

When you think about a court, judges and lawyers might come to mind first. Courts often rely on everyday citizens, too. A jury is a group of people from the community. They listen to **evidence** and make a decision. Juries make some of the most important decisions in American courts.

Serving on a jury is a **civic duty**. The U.S. jury system developed over many years. It helps make certain that government officials do not misuse their power and that trials are fair.

The Unified Judicial System of Pennsylvania puts it this way: "To ensure their rights, the people themselves must be willing to play a role in the justice system."

HISTORIC ROOTS

Many legal words come from other languages. "Jury" can be tracked to a Latin term meaning "to swear" or "to take an oath." Jurors take an oath to judge fairly.

Before hearing evidence, members of a jury, called jurors, promise to consider the law and the facts of the case.

TYPES OF LEGAL CASES

There are several different types of legal cases. Civil cases are between two or more individuals, including **plaintiffs** and **defendants**. The plaintiff starts the legal case, accusing the defendant of causing some sort of harm. The plaintiff asks the court to stop the defendant or make the defendant pay.

Criminal cases are brought to court by the government. A **prosecutor**, on behalf of the government, accuses someone of breaking the law. Under United States law, a person is considered to be innocent until proven guilty. It's up to the prosecutor to prove to a jury that a person committed a crime.

Sometimes, the two sides come to an agreement outside the court. Other times, judges make a decision regarding the case. But in many important cases, a jury makes the final decision.

Jim Obergefell was a plaintiff who said he was harmed when the state of Ohio would not recognize his marriage to another man. In 2015, the U.S. Supreme Court agreed, allowing same-sex couples to marry in all 50 states.

TYPES OF JURIES

There are two types of juries: grand juries and trial juries. Grand juries are "grand" because they include more people than trial juries, between 16 and 23. Trial juries, sometimes called petit juries, usually have 6 to 12 people. *Petit* is French for "small."

A grand jury considers evidence that government prosecutors bring to a criminal case. The grand jury decides whether the government has good reason to put the accused person on trial. Grand juries may also investigate other matters.

This trial jury heard a case against Albert Fall, who was U.S. secretary of the interior in the 1920s. They found him guilty of taking bribes.

Trial juries can be involved in criminal or civil cases. Trial juries in criminal cases listen to the evidence and decide whether the accused person broke the law. Juries in civil cases decide whether the defendant caused harm to the plaintiff.

HISTORY OF THE JURY TRIAL

In the Middle Ages, much of Europe used "trial by ordeal." An accused person faced an ordeal, or danger such as drowning, fire, or combat. Making it through was seen as a sign of innocence. Starting in the early 1200s, this began to be replaced by early juries. These were councils of men asked to look into legal cases. Over time, they were called to decide more cases.

The Magna Carta, an English legal document, or formal piece of writing, from 1215, said an accused person couldn't be imprisoned or lose property except "by lawful judgment of his peers."

The American jury system grew out of English traditions. In 1623, settlers in what would become Massachusetts created a law "that all criminal facts, and also matters . . . between man and man should be tried by the **verdict** of twelve honest men . . . in form of a jury."

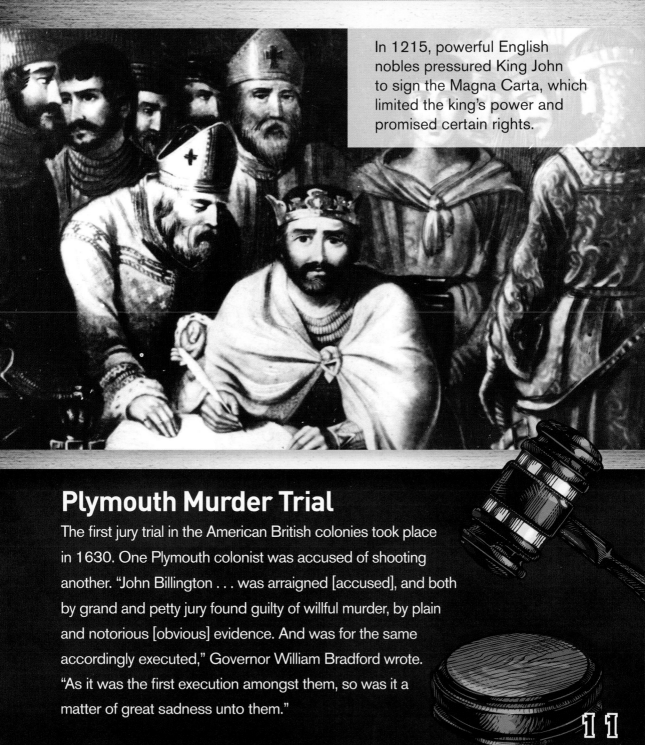

In 1215, powerful English nobles pressured King John to sign the Magna Carta, which limited the king's power and promised certain rights.

Plymouth Murder Trial

The first jury trial in the American British colonies took place in 1630. One Plymouth colonist was accused of shooting another. "John Billington . . . was arraigned [accused], and both by grand and petty jury found guilty of willful murder, by plain and notorious [obvious] evidence. And was for the same accordingly executed," Governor William Bradford wrote. "As it was the first execution amongst them, so was it a matter of great sadness unto them."

11

American colonial juries sometimes showed independence from English leaders. In the 1730s, John Peter Zenger printed newspaper articles criticizing William Cosby, the royal governor of New York. Cosby brought Zenger to trial on charges of libel, the legal term for harming a person's **reputation** through the written word.

Zenger's lawyer, Andrew Hamilton, admitted that Zenger had printed the articles. Hamilton said the important thing was that the information Zenger had printed was true. The jury agreed and decided that Zenger was not guilty. This decision helped to build up the idea of a free press.

Later, colonial juries refused to convict people charged with breaking unpopular English laws. In 1776, the Declaration of Independence blamed the king for "**depriving** us in many cases, of the benefit of Trial by Jury."

American colonists saw the Zenger trial as proof that juries could protect the rights of the people.

13

AN IMPARTIAL JURY

The founders of the United States saw the right to a jury trial as important to protecting American freedom. The Constitution, the Bill of Rights, and state laws all set rules for trial by jury. The Seventh Amendment promises the right to trial by jury in federal civil cases.

For criminal cases, the Sixth Amendment promises "the right to a speedy and public trial, by an **impartial** jury of the State and district wherein the crime shall have been committed." Members of the jury should come to the case with a fair point of view.

The U.S. Supreme Court has said that to be impartial, a jury should be made up of "a representative cross section of the community."

Who Are a Person's Peers?

Over time, courts have changed their positions on who should serve on a jury. In the 1880 decision in *Strauder v. West Virginia*, the Supreme Court said states could not ban black men from juries, since that would **discriminate** against black citizens accused of crimes.

Jurors are picked from a larger group of citizens. Judges and lawyers for both sides can ask questions before the members of a jury are chosen.

THE GRAND JURY

The Fifth Amendment requires grand juries before most major federal criminal trials. Some states regularly use grand juries to decide whether criminal cases should go to trial. In other states, a judge usually makes that decision.

A grand jury hears evidence in secret. The prosecutor shares information to back up the government's accusation that a person committed a crime. The grand jury can hear from several witnesses in a case, but the person who is accused doesn't present a defense.

Some judges and lawyers say that grand juries go along with prosecutors too often. They worry the process is one sided.

One grand jury may decide on many cases. Federal grand jury duty usually lasts for about 18 months. A serving juror will hear evidence about once a week.

WHERE'S THE JUDGE?

A grand jury doesn't spend much time with a judge. The role of the judge is usually just bringing the grand jury together and having jurors take their oath.

Organized crime figure Aniello Dellacroce (right) was called to speak to a grand jury in Queens, New York, in 1971. Dellacroce refused to answer any questions, and was sent to jail for a year.

PROBABLE CAUSE

A grand jury doesn't judge whether a person is guilty or innocent of a crime. The job of a grand jury is to decide whether there is enough evidence that a crime was committed. This is called "probable cause."

More than half the grand jury needs to come to agreement in order to make a decision. If a grand jury decides that there is probable cause that a crime was committed, it writes up a "true bill." The accused person is then indicted, or formally charged with a crime. The case can then head to trial.

Other Roles of Grand Juries

Grand juries are used in different ways in different states. Many states have grand juries that look for **corruption** in government. Others have grand juries that inspect jails and prisons. Some grand juries are asked to explore issues of public interest. They have the power to make people hand over evidence and the power to have witnesses speak. These powers help grand juries investigate these things.

TOO EASY?

Most times, grand juries will agree to prosecutors' requests.
New York Judge Sol Wachtler once complained that a prosecutor could
get a grand jury to "indict a ham sandwich."

Many protesters marched in 2015 after a grand jury didn't indict police officer Timothy Loehmann in the shooting death of 12-year-old Tamir Rice.

If the grand jury doesn't think there is probable cause, it writes up a "no bill." The accused person isn't charged with a crime.

THE TRIAL JURY

A trial jury hears from two sides in a process run by a judge. Both sides can bring in witnesses and present their arguments to the court. Most parts of the trial are public, but the jury makes its decision in private.

Criminal trials usually have 12 jurors. In many civil trials, just six people sit on the jury. A judge can also decide to have an alternate juror. An alternate juror will listen to evidence for the entire trial but helps decide the verdict only if another juror has to leave.

The 14th Amendment

States have different legal standards than the federal government. The 14th Amendment, adopted in 1868, says states cannot "deprive any person of life, liberty, or property, without due process of law." In the 1968 *Duncan v. Louisiana* decision, the Supreme Court said Fifth and Sixth Amendment jury trial rights apply to states, too. "Trial by jury in criminal cases is fundamental to the American scheme of justice," the court said.

Bartolomeo Vanzetti and Nicola Sacco were Italian immigrants who were executed after being convicted of a 1920 murder. Critics thought jurors were **biased** against Sacco and Vanzetti's political views and foreign background.

Laws protect jurors from losing their jobs if they miss time at work. It's also illegal to influence a jury's decision by writing to or talking to a juror outside of the trial.

DECIDING ON FACTS

A trial jury decides what the facts of a case are, based on the evidence presented by both sides and the laws that apply to the case. Then jury members vote on a verdict.

In a civil case, the verdict is in favor of the plaintiff or defendant. If the jury decides the defendant caused harm, then the defendant needs to make up for that harm.

Former football player O. J. Simpson was accused of killing his ex-wife and her friend. In a 1995 trial, the jury thought there was reasonable doubt and found him not guilty.

In a criminal case, the verdict says whether the accused person is guilty. The prosecutor's job in court is to provide proof "beyond reasonable doubt" that the defendant broke the law. It's not enough for a jury to think that a defendant probably committed a crime. A jury should be very sure before giving a guilty verdict.

PICKING JURORS

The process of creating a jury starts with a list of people who live in the area. Court officials chose names at random from the list. The group chosen is called the jury pool. The people picked for jury duty come to court. There, the judge and the lawyers from both sides can ask questions. They want to make sure jurors can consider a case fairly.

Women in the Jury Box

As women won the right to vote, more states allowed them to serve on juries. However, many states still treated women differently when it came to jury service. In its 1975 *Taylor v. Louisiana* decision, the Supreme Court struck down systems that left many women out of the jury pool. The court again said that juries should come from a representative cross section of the community.

These women made up California's first all-female jury in 1911. The editor of the *Watts News* was charged with printing bad language. The jury's verdict was not guilty.

There are many reasons someone might not be able to join a jury. If a juror knows someone in the case or has a personal connection to it, a lawyer can ask a judge to remove that juror. Lawyers can also remove a certain number of jurors without giving a reason, but they shouldn't discriminate based on race or gender.

PARTS OF A TRIAL

Once a jury is picked, jurors take an oath to be fair and follow the law. The judge explains what is expected of the jury.

Next, lawyers for both sides have the chance to make their opening statements, explaining their point of view on the case. Both sides can bring in witnesses, question each other's witnesses, and offer evidence to the court. A criminal defendant doesn't have to **testify** but can choose to do so.

Both sides have a chance to give closing arguments. The judge gives instructions to the jury on the laws that matter to the case and what the jury needs to consider in making its decision. The jury leaves to talk it over and then returns with a decision. Jury decisions may take some time as jurors work together to come to an agreement.

"YOUR HONOR, I OBJECT!"

If a question is unfair or something given as evidence isn't allowed, a lawyer can object. The judge can tell the jury not to pay attention to that evidence.

Judge Christine McEvoy gives instructions to the jury in a Massachusetts murder trial.

MAKING A DECISION

The judge or jury names a jury foreperson. The foreperson is in charge of making sure each member of the jury has a say when it's time to make a decision. The foreperson shares the jury's verdict with the court.

The process of coming to a jury decision is called deliberation. The members of the jury go over the evidence they heard and tell each other their views. In most cases, juries must make a **unanimous** decision on the verdict.

When jurors think they won't ever be able to agree, it's called a hung jury. This leads to a **mistrial**. Sometimes the case ends there. To continue, the prosecutor or plaintiff must start the trial over again, bringing the case to a new jury.

AVOIDING INTERFERENCE

A judge can have the jury sequestered. This means jurors are kept separate from other people, even their families. This is supposed to help them reach a fair verdict without outside influences.

Foreperson Oscar Criner speaks in 2002 after his jury found the accounting firm Arthur Andersen guilty of interfering with a federal investigation. The Supreme Court later said that the judge had given bad instructions to the jury.

A CRUCIAL ROLE

The American jury system began with English legal traditions but has grown and changed. Ordinary citizens from a cross section of the community make some of the most important decisions in our courts.

This does have dangers. Sometimes jurors are biased, or they aren't able to understand the law or the evidence in a case. Sometimes they make the wrong decision. However, the jury system is meant to make sure everyone gets a fair trial. Often, having a jury protects the rights of the people. The nation's founders saw this as so important that jury rules are in the Bill of Rights.

Jurors take an oath to consider the evidence and try to make a fair judgment. Our courts rely on them to keep that promise.

GLOSSARY

biased: Having a tendency to believe that some people or ideas are better than others.

civic duty: A responsibility a person has to their community.

corruption: Illegal or dishonest behavior, especially by people in power.

defendant: Someone accused of a crime or someone who's being sued in a civil trial.

deprive: To deny.

discriminate: To treat people unequally based on class, race, religion, or other factors.

evidence: Something that shows that something else is true.

impartial: Treating all sides equally.

mistrial: A trial that ends because of an error or without a verdict.

plaintiff: Someone who brings a lawsuit against another person.

prosecutor: A lawyer who prosecutes, or argues charges against, an accused person in court.

reputation: The way someone is thought of by other people.

testify: To speak or answer questions in a court of law.

unanimous: Agreed to by everyone.

verdict: Judgment or decision.

INDEX

WEBSITES

Due to the changing nature of Internet links, PowerKids Press has developed an online list of
websites related to the subject of this book. This site is updated regularly. Please use this link to
access the list: www.powerkidslinks.com/courts/juries